HOW TO UNMASK
AND OVERCOME FEAR

Dr. Janell Jones

Copyright © 2020 by Melanin Grace Publishing, LLC

All rights reserved. No part of this publication may be reproduced, distributed or transmitted in any form or by any means, including photocopying, recording, or other electronic or mechanical methods, without the prior written permission of the publisher, except in the case of brief quotations embodied in critical reviews and certain other noncommercial uses permitted by copyright law. For permission requests, write to the publisher, addressed "Attention: Permissions Coordinator," at the address below.

Melanin Grace Publishing, LLC
P.O. Box 714
Pickerington, OH 43147

ISBN-978-1-7336439-2-4

Disclaimer

The information provided in this book is not a substitute for professional advice or therapy. The author makes no legal claims, and the material is not intended to replace the services of a certified professional.

Welcome!

Message from the author

Thank you for purchasing the F$#% Book! I challenge you to go beyond simply reading this book and identify your own fears and overcome them. At the end of this book, there is a FREE worksheet (with video instructions) to help unmask and overcome your fear(s). You will have to subscibe to receive the download---but it's well worth it.

Table Of Contents

Introduction _____ 6
Chapter 1: Fear Factor _____ 8
Chapter 2: When in Doubt _____ 12
Chapter 3: Worry/Anxiety _____ 15
Chapter 4: Issa Insecurity _____ 20
Chapter 5: The Green-Eyed Bandits
Jealousy/Envy _____ 23
Chapter 6: The P's of Fear
Procrastination/Perfectionism _____ 25
Chapter 7: Approval Seeking _____ 29
Chapter 8: To Fear or Not to Fear
The fear of failure/fear of success _____ 34
Chapter 9: Overcoming fear _____ 38
Additional Resources _____ 45
About The Author _____ 46

Introduction

For many years, I knew there was more on the inside of me. I remember being twelve years old, my friend and I were sitting on the couch in the living room, and some stranger who was visiting my house told me I was going to be great when I grew up. I hadn't ever heard that before. This stranger telling me I was going to be great was music to my ears because I had big dreams, but it also brought fear to the rest of my body.

I carried for years—this big dream inside of me but didn't know how I would accomplish it. Everything happening in my life held me back from attaining it: living in poverty, teenage pregnancy, divorce, and custody battles. What I couldn't understand was how people who faced similar adversity (or any adversity) were able to live their dreams but I was still wishing for mine. It was easy to say that people like Tyler Perry, or Oprah Winfrey are extremely successful but they have been through some crap. If they are significant role models in our society and were able to overcome adversity, what the heck is wrong with me? Surely, God is no respecter of persons.

As I went on my self-discovery journey, I realized one of the biggest, most debilitating problems causing me to not fulfill my purpose was fear. It wasn't just fear, it was all its hidden triggers too.

We are going to unmask fear and learn how to overcome it.

Let the journey begin.

Chapter 1
Fear Factor

When you hear the word fear, what comes to mind? We all know the feeling as making our skin crawl, or we picture someone hiding in a corner somewhere when faced with a scary situation. Let's take a deeper dive at fear.

Throughout this book, I will be using the dictionary to break down words. It's a great way to learn the anatomy of a word so that we can truly understand its meaning.

According to Dictionary.com, fear is an **unpleasant emotion** caused by the **belief** that some person or thing is **dangerous** and is likely to cause **pain** or be a **threat.**

Let's start with "unpleasant emotion." The beginning of fear is a feeling; the feeling that something isn't right or uncomfortable. This feeling causes paralysis. We all have had dreams where we couldn't move our feet toward progress. Have you ever tried to pursue your dreams and an uncomfortable feeling overtakes you? There is a difference between discernment and fear. The definition of discernment is "the ability to judge well." In Christian contexts, discernment is described as "perception in the absence of judgement with a view of obtaining spiritual guidance and understanding." I have seen so many people, including myself, not take action toward their dreams because of this feeling. They try to rationalize by saying stuff like "I am waiting on God" or "I just don't feel right" and put it off as discernment, when in reality, it's fear. Your discernment is necessary, but don't masquerade your feelings of fear as discernment.

Next is belief… if you don't get anything from this book, get this: your mindset is everything. You have this unpleasant feeling that stems from your thoughts. This makes me ask: What are you thinking; what are your underlying beliefs? I believe that 80% of what we do is mindset and 20% is action. If you don't believe that you are worthy or you can't achieve your dreams, then you will not. This is true for whatever you are trying to do.

When we are faced with danger, human nature causes us to respond with fight or flight. "Fight or flight" is psychological response and was coined by Walter Cannon in the 1920's. Cannon believed that when an individual is faced with a threatening situation, their response is usually to run (flight) or face (fight) the problem. Both of them can cause our bodies to respond in an unhealthy way, which can produce physical illness, especially over time. I heard ambulance sirens as I was writing this. The immediate danger presenting itself is safety for my daughter who just left for school, and my husband who just left for the gym. It didn't help that my dog jumped up and barked. My first thought was to call them. My heart starting racing at the assumption they might be in danger.

In reality, most of what we believe is true danger isn't real. It is in our minds, but we respond the same as if it were reality. That is what happens with our dreams.

We have these big ideas, but when faced with putting action with our dreams and plans, we immediately begin to fear.

I believe there are many masks of fear: anxiety, worry, doubt, envy, insecurity, procrastination, perfectionism, approval-seeking, fear of failing, and fear of succeeding. We are going to unmask each of them and learn how to overcome.

Chapter 2
When in Doubt

When I searched the word "doubt" in the Merriam-Webster Dictionary, the synonym was fear in the verb sense. We all know that a verb means action. Therefore, doubt and fear are one in the same. The noun doubt means uncertainty. Looking back at the definition of fear, it is brought on by an unpleasant emotion. Uncertainty is definitely unpleasant. Uncertainty makes a person feel unstable and out of control. People typically don't do well when they feel they are not in control of their lives. To compensate, they often begin to try to control everything—and I do mean *everything*—around them.

This usually creates panic and poor decision making, making matters worse.

When we doubt, we don't believe things will happen that'll work in our favor. This can be external or internal circumstances. We doubt that we'll get that job, that our dreams will come true, that we'll succeed in college, or get married. These are things we put on our vision boards and our to-do list, but we don't truly believe they will happen. This is how doubt rears its ugly head. Doubt will say you can desire these things—but do you really deserve them? Why you? Will this really happen for you?

I am going to take a minute and go to the story in the bible when Jesus healed a boy who had a dumb or foul spirit. The father pleaded with Jesus to remove the spirit. He said that he tried everything. The foul spirit tossed the boy in the fire and the water. Jesus said to the father, "You have little faith, and all things are possible for those who believe." The father replied, "I believe but help my unbelief." Essentially, he is saying; I believe you but help my doubt—my uncertainty. I want nothing more than to believe that my son is healed,

BUT my circumstances are screaming louder than my beliefs. What I am seeing is screaming more than my faith. All Jesus was asking is to believe.

When we doubt, we stop believing that things will work out for us. We keep throwing the big BUT in there. Our job is to simply believe, which means to trust that it will work. If you have any doubts, do like the father in the bible—ask for help. We are humans who experience real emotions. If you are in a situation where you don't get what you think you deserve, believe you will achieve something better. Have you ever experienced a time when you believed God for something major. You were praying, fasting, and confessing that it was yours. Then, you didn't get it. You were probably disappointed initially, but when you looked back on your life, you were so happy that you didn't get that opportunity, you dodged a bullet. You have to trust the process. When you are believing for something, also believe that God has the best for you.

Chapter 3
Worry/Anxiety

Worrying is a dream killer. Have you ever been so worried about something you couldn't function? You couldn't think clearly, you couldn't sleep or eat because you were consumed with an event or a thing. Let's break the definition down further. To worry is to give in to anxiety or unease; allowing one's mind to dwell on difficulty or trouble.

Typically, when we worry, our minds immediately go to the worst-case scenario. Think about it, have you ever been up all night worrying because you felt good about a situation? Were you up all night because you knew that you were going to get the job, be accepted to a college, make the team, or get the contract? Absolutely not, you were thinking about the no's and what if's. You dwell in the space of uncertainty and it's usually negative. ***There is a difference between worry and anticipation. It's like a child at Christmas. They are expecting something great to happen between the time they go to bed and the time they wake up. They know that something great is waiting for them.***

Anxiety and worry breed with each other. They often go hand and hand. There are many people who have worried so much, they had an anxiety attack. As a counselor, I've had several clients diagnosed with anxiety disorder. Just like worry, they feel their lives are out of control. This causes their bodies to over respond, and all of a sudden, the symptoms manifest. They can't breathe. You've seen it on TV plenty of times. What's the first thing they go for? The brown paper bag. Anxiety is the feeling of nervousness or unease, typically about an imminent event or something with an unclear outcome.

When these negative thoughts bombard your

mind, they become mental threats which induce fear. This unpleasant emotion leaves you with no resolve. You play the scenario over and over again in your mind. One thing I know about worrying is if you don't process it properly, you'll be 90 years old still worrying. An example of this is my mother. I love her to pieces, but she worries a lot. Let me take you on a day journey of her worrying. First, she had a doctor's appointment at 10:15 am. She called her neighbor the night before and asked her to wake her up at 6 am. Because she worried all night, she was up at 5 am. I have to assume she was worried about missing her appointment. Her ride came to pick her up around 9:30 am. She was waiting for him around 8 am. She returned home from her doctor's appointment so I could take her to the hair salon at 2:30 pm. It takes approximately 20 minutes to get to the salon from my house. We left my house at 1:50 pm to stop at the bank which is in route to the salon. We get in the car, and she starts panicking, saying she left something. For five minutes, she was concerned about what she left.

Everything that came out of her mouth was negative. Immediately, she went to the worst-case scenario. Then, she found what she was looking for in her purse. We went to the bank and got her some money. We hit the freeway, and she said we were going to be late. I could tell she was hesitant to say it at first because she knew I would tell her to calm down, which I did. She's my mother; I knew she was assuming we were going to be late. Do you know what time we go to the salon? 2:17 pm. We were actually early. On our way home, I had to stop to pick up a few things for her. As we were getting close to her apartment, she starts to panic again. She couldn't find her keys. She started thinking, how will I get in my house. I had a parent-teacher conference that night so I couldn't hang out much longer. Instead of taking her home, I jumped lanes so I could go home and get my children for the PTC. Then, she found her keys on the side of her. She'd pulled them out previously and they must have slipped.

I learned many lessons from this. Instead of freaking out, take a moment to breathe. Don't jump to the worst thing that could happen when you're in a jam. Understand that worrying can be passed down generationally. We often learn from our environment. If we see our parents panicking at any given moment, chances are, we will do the same. I have noticed that most people in my family worry and automatically assumes the worst. When you panic, you cause everyone around you to do the same. You are creating added stress that you don't need. In the end, everything worked out. Remember the flight or fight? It is the response to your situation; you are causing your body to respond. This ultimately has a physical effect on your body that results in sickness.

In this example, what was the worst that could happen? She would have been late for the doctors? She could reschedule. They usually have a policy that allows patients to be at least 15 minutes late. She would have been late for the salon? I would've texted the hairdresser to let her know, and we wouldn't have been too late. She couldn't find her keys? I have a key to her apartment. We would have had to contact the neighbor to enter the front door, but we had a key to the apartment. She spent so much time worrying that she couldn't enjoy herself. I have been guilty of this too.

Chapter 4
Issa Insecurity

You are probably wondering how insecurity is a facet of fear. Insecurity is defined as; not confident or assured; uncertain and anxious. Do you see that? Uncertain and anxious—sounds familiar, right?

While doubt focuses on the external and/or internal circumstance, insecurity focuses on how you feel about and see yourself. The most basic of needs for a human to function properly is security. We need to know we are safe to feel and think how we do, that we have somewhere safe to lay our heads. Insecurity screams "I am not enough; it is not safe for me to do this." At some point, an experience or a person told us that we were not enough. We took that and incorporated it in our beliefs. This can be something as small as a gym teacher telling you that you are fat, and the result is you struggling with your weight for 20 years. You've imbedded that you are fat in your mind. Therefore, your actions follow your beliefs.

Insecurity will have you comparing yourself to other people and not fully developing yourself. You'll see others as a threat and then diminish either that person or yourself. I see women do this all the time; I've even been guilty of it. We see a beautiful woman enter the room. We try to find something wrong with her in order to build ourselves up. That, or we will focus on the great qualities she has and belittle ourselves. Comparing yourself with others will highjack your destiny. You are saying to yourself that what the other person has appears to be better (even when you are putting them down), and you'd rather be them instead of fully being yourself. This is why knowing yourself is very important, because you can't walk in 100% authenticity if you don't know who you are.

The truth about insecurity is that everyone deals with it. I believe people deal with it when they're in certain or new situations and they lack confidence. The other type is when insecurity is entrenched in a person's character. This person usually lacks confidence in everything they do. Because we can't walk away from our character, this type of insecurity requires a different approach. The situationally insecure person usually has an easier time bouncing back. The person who has insecurity as a character trait is going to require more work. This person will be required to change their mindset on a consistent basis in order to transform their mind.

Chapter 5

The Green-Eyed Bandits

Jealousy/Envy

The green-eyed bandit is right here, jealousy and envy. Jealousy and envy are like two fish in a pond—while they're different, they're bound to swim together. For this definition, I'll use a sermon that I heard in church. The Pastor stated that jealousy is when you are hating on someone else for what they have, whereas envy is when you are worried about someone taking what you have. An example of jealousy is hating that your friend or family member received a deal from a TV station to produce a show. This was on your wish list, but it hasn't happened yet. You smile, but inside, you are wondering why nothing like that has happened to you. Envy is more like you have a man and you see a confident woman walk by and you start to feel a certain type of way. One is wanting; hating on something someone else has; the other is you having something and hating because you think someone will steal it.

Jealousy and envy are rooted in fear. Essentially, you are saying that you are not good enough and you are afraid you never will be, otherwise, why would it matter that someone is else is doing well? You fear that you will never rise to the level of confidence, wealth, relationship, or whatever, so you wish you had what the other person had or you are afraid they will take what you have. Which, internally, makes you feel unworthy or—insecure.

Chapter 6
The P's of Fear
Procrastination/Perfectionism

We all know that procrastination is putting something off, but do you know it can be fear based? Now, some people are simply just lazy and poor planners, but a lot of times, if you dig deep enough, you will find that fear is really governing why a person is procrastinating. Outside of being lazy, people procrastinate because of fear. The fear is screaming at them that it won't work, their idea is stupid, that someone has that idea already. If I believe my idea won't work, deep down inside, why would I take the time to invest in it? I have heard so many people come up with excellent ideas. People who are skilled at what they do. They will find a hundred reasons for why they can't do it.

Fear causes you to put it off because you are afraid of the uncertainty. I am always baffled at people who complain about their situation but are not taking any efforts to do anything about it. I am not good at listening to people talk about what they are going to do, I need to see some action. When I hear people like this, I know that the real reason they are not pursuing their dream is because they are afraid. Fear will make you believe that you can't move, so… you don't.

Perfectionism. Why in the world would I put this in here? How can making sure everything is right equated to fear? I am very glad that you asked. A lot of people look at perfectionism as a positive attribute. There is nothing wrong with doing your best and striving for greatness… perfectionism isn't that. Fear is rooted in perfectionism because a person will replicate a process until they get it right, until it's perfect. This causes a person to never launch. Often times, the deep-rooted issue is not that they are waiting for it to be perfect, they are afraid to jump. Questions bombard their minds; what happens if I fail, will people like this, am I going to be judged, is this going to work? These questions cause paralysis that is hidden by the excuse of perfectionism. The truth is, there will never be a perfect time. There are so many companies who "test" their products prior to launching them. There are also so many companies who launch their products with errors. This can range from technical difficulties to grammatical errors. Do you know what these companies do when they find these mistakes? Fix them.

It is true, people will stand by the sidelines critiquing your mistakes, telling you that something is not right with what you are trying to do. There are also people who are willing to help you with this. Understand that you are not great in everything and—surprise—you are a flawed human being. I read Gary V's book *Crushing It,* and he talked about the difference between when he first started making YouTube videos vs now. He stated that his first videos were horrible. He didn't have the equipment, the lighting, he used terminology that others wouldn't understand (he started off in the wine business). As time went on, he began to change his equipment, be comfortable with the camera, and most importantly, be himself. If you are starting a project and you know someone else who is good in a certain area, delegate it. Know your strengths and run with that. Don't hold yourself up because you are waiting for everything to line up. Whatever your goal is, when you start to move toward it, you will gain clarity. This will allow you to "upgrade" along the way.

Chapter 7
Approval Seeking

I believe as humans we want some type of recognition. This doesn't mean you do things to get recognized, but it is nice to hear your kids say thank you, your husband buy you flowers, or your employer promote you at your job. No one wants to feel undervalued, especially if you have worked hard to get where you are. There is nothing wrong with wanting to be appreciated. However, some people seek approval out of fear because they think if someone validates them, it's accepted, and then they can proceed. It's almost like they are asking for permission to move forward when deep down inside, they are afraid. They have many creative ideas, some even have the ambition to implement them, but fear stops them in their track.

Let me make a disclaimer here. There is absolutely nothing wrong with having a mentor or a coach. However, if you have a mentor or a coach, this is usually someone who is where you want to be. This is not a friend or family member who you always send ideas to so they can approve. If you are seeking advice, level up to someone who has done what you want to do. If you seek advice from someone who is not where you want to be, it's the blind leading the blind.

You can have a life-changing idea but will not share it with the world because you are afraid. You then take that idea to a friend or family member who doesn't have the same vision as you, and they will either try to tell you what to do if it were them or won't be able to provide you with the full picture of what you need. A lot of times when you have a vision, it's your vision. The best thing you can do is really ask God what to do with it. Once you receive guidance, ask Him to put people in your life to help you carry it out.

I had a bad habit of sharing my ideas with people who were either where I was or not implementing at all. I am talking about the infancy of ideas. I was sharing for approval to launch. When people say I shouldn't or I was are doing too much, I wouldn't launch. I was afraid that because they didn't like it, it wouldn't work. I would get discouraged and toss the idea. What I have learned to do is share when I am beyond the infancy stage. I allow my creative juices to flow uninterrupted. It can still be challenging because I get excited when I have new ideas. I also recognized strength in certain people and would only get advice from them if their gift called for it. During the infancy stage of a creation, I learned to ask someone with experience. You still must seek God, especially if the idea is a direct deposit from God. There are many people who shared their ideas and were laughed at. They pursued it anyway and became successful. Companies like Amazon, Apple, and Netflix are great examples of people pursuing in spite of people telling people they weren't going anywhere.

Don't ever believe that you have too many ideas. You will have to learn to prioritize your ideas, but they were placed on the inside of you for a reason. Find out what you love to do and what you are good at. Sometimes your purpose is different from your skills, sometimes they correlate. For instance, you made be good with fixing computers but you love to sing. There is no law that says you can't do both. This is why it's very important to not allow people to limit you.

Don't be afraid to share your ideas with the world once you're out of the infancy stage. Don't seek approval, seek advice or help. Some of your ideas will have to be done silently. This can be scary, but you can certainly do things to make sure your audience approves and not just your friends. For instance, I am writing this book. This is probably my seventh book that I have started. I have completed and published two books. I already have the cover for this book that I will poll my audience with to see what they think prior to finishing the book. I'll do some research to see what others have to say about the topic of fear. I know there is a lot of information out there because fear is one of the greatest stealers of life. I am hoping that my book is different because I dive deep into the many facets of fear. This time, I didn't tell a lot of people that I was working on this book. I told *maybe* three before the whole world knew. In fact, this book sat in silence for two years.

Chapter 8

To Fear or Not to Fear
The fear of failure/fear of success

The fear of failure and success is always interesting to me. I have had a lot of people say that they understand the fear of failure but who in the world would be afraid of success. When John Maxwell wrote the book *Failing Forward*, it was a relief because so many people didn't know how to asses failure. They often internalized it and never tried anything with a risk again, or low risk. Failing is not a great feeling. You did all this work, you put all your energy, time, and money into something, and you are not getting a return on your investment. Money and maybe energy can be replaced, but time cannot. Then... it didn't work. When you first started the adventure (new job, business, marriage, family, invention, etc.), you were super excited. Eventually, after feeling defeated, you quit, or wanted to.

The truth about failure is it's inevitable, everyone fails. The key is how you perceive failure that will create success or reproduce failure. If you really look at every successful person—go ahead and take your pick—you will find that ALL of them failed at something. From Thomas Edison to Jim Carey. Often times, what appears to be an overnight success is really a lengthy process. You have some stories of people who went from one end of the spectrum to the other, those are the outliers. For most of us, it took a lot longer and was a process. Some people even give up. However, for the most part, people who succeed have been investing in something for a long time before they see true fruits of success.

My definition of the fear of failure is simply being afraid to put yourself out there. When you invest in yourself and you are doing something dear to your heart, you are being vulnerable. The world is a scary place to trust with your vulnerability. You can be judged or ridiculed for something you are very passionate about. Who in their right mind wants to be rejected by the world? No one. So many people become crippled just by the idea of rejection. Remember that fear arises from the belief of something dangerous. When a person starts to think of being rejected, they shut their ideas down because it's perceived as dangerous.

Allow me to add a side note here. If you have any issues with rejection, I strongly recommend dealing with that sooner rather than later. If we have childhood or adulthood rejection issues, we see through the lens of rejection. So when you are moving forward in reaching your dreams, the same feeling of rejection you had as a child arises. This will cause you to back away from pursing your dreams because you will get triggered and associate with those old feelings. You have to deal with them if you want to be successful.

The fear of failure or success is frightening because you are venturing into the unknown. Many people make declarations and claim they want to go to the next level but are afraid to get there. There are certain things one must do to get to the next level. I don't believe that you have to change your personality to get there, but I do believe there is some character development that needs to take place. For instance, when I was a single mother, I use to shop at this really cheap clothing store. The material was thin, and the clothes would only last a year, if that. It was what I could afford at that time. After about seven years of finally being financially stable, I was able to shop at higher priced stores. To my surprise, I really enjoyed the quality of the clothes. They were lasting several years instead of several months. I would talk to my family and would say that a shirt was $39 and they would say that was too expensive.

When we transition to success, you may have to pay more, dump a few friends or family members, hang with different circles of people, and go to different and unfamiliar places. The discomfort of that is why we are truly afraid of success, because we don't want to be uncomfortable. We get so cozy in our comfort zones that it can cost us.

Chapter 9
Overcoming fear

Now that we understand the definitions of fear, doubt, worry/anxiety, jealousy/envy, and procrastination/perfectionism, approval seeking, and the fear of failure and success, let's talk about how to overcome them. If you look at the definition of each word, you will see a common factor: uncertainty. Most often, we are paralyzed by fear because we are uncertain about ourselves, situations, places, or others. We've imbedded uncertainty in our beliefs, which becomes our thinking. Our thinking controls our world. Have you ever been afraid of something that isn't true but it's real in your mind. For instance, you are on your way to work and you don't remember if you left the flat iron on in your bathroom. Your mind begins to play different scenarios in your mind which consumes your thoughts. By this time, you are closer to work, but because you don't want your house to burn down, you turn around and head back home. When you get home and run upstairs to your bathroom, you realize not only did you turn the flat iron off, you wrapped the cord around it and put it under the bathroom sink. The entire time you were driving to work, your heart was racing.

Get your mind right. Remember, what you focus on will expand and eventually manifest. This is the power of our mind. You are going to have uncomfortable moments and be in unpleasant situations. This is life. As difficult as it may be, you have to find a way to not allow the negative thoughts to overtake you. You will have to deal with your feelings—don't ignore them. That will not help either. Be honest about how you feel. If you are afraid of something, express it. However, take another action to overcome it. Meditate, which means to practice something over and over on the positive. If you are uncertain about something, just believe that things will work out in your favor. If someone tells you no, move on. Practice mindfulness. Mindfulness meditation allows you to focus on the here and now. This is good if you are dealing with anxiety. You're able to process your thoughts without judgement. There are several videos that teach how to use mindfulness in your everyday life. Understand that a lot of times, fear exists in your mind. Remember, it's caused by a belief.

Do it afraid! Now, let me share what I have learned about fear so far and the many facets that it has. Learn from those who are successful. I guarantee that you will find that they failed at something or had a feeling of fear when they were stepping out of their comfort zone. Despite their feelings, they pursued their dreams anyway. They did it afraid. You have to toss that emotion of fear away and jump. You have to stop automatically assuming the worst and go for it. Don't over analyze it, or, simply put, don't worry about it. When you spend time worrying about it, you are replacing faith with fear.

Be consistent. This has been a very hard lesson for

me. After I was in the game of building my business, I began to hear people say be consistent. At first, I was like, yes, here is my schedule, and then when I would do something that people had to show up for, and no one showed up, defeat replaced consistency. I would spend two weeks or a month doing nothing but sulking in the defeat. I wasn't hurting anyone but myself. Then I would get motivated by an idea and start all over again. Unfortunately, when I started over, the momentum died, and I truly had to start all over. It wasn't until about a year and a half later when I fully understood this concept that no one knows who you are but if you show up consistently, they will know.

Don't allow disappointment to stop you. Let me make another side note here—don't depend on people you know to support your vision like you'd hoped. You will have people close to you who will support you, however, it will not carry you to the level you need to be. You are going to have to venture out, network, get familiar with software or hire someone to help you build your dreams. Remember, your purpose is your responsibility.

How to Unmask and Overcome Fear

Listen, my dear…YOU ARE ENOUGH. Take a moment and say that out loud—I AM ENOUGH. Okay, say it again… Insecurity, jealousy, and envy will make you think you're not. This false belief will have you lower your standards just because you don't see your value. God has placed everything you need on the inside of you. Like a muscle, you have to continue to work to define it. Oftentimes, this process of working out isn't easy and can be dreadful. But by the end, your body is defined, dopamine is released—creating a feeling of pleasure and reward, eating habits are better, and your overall mental and physical health improves. There are some things that will take longer, and that's okay. Don't think if you plant a seed today, you'll see the fruit tomorrow.

Operate in wisdom, not perfection. As I mentioned before, we are all flawed. I understand this can be challenging if you grew up with a critical parent or people who made you feel like you did nothing right. This is where you challenge your mindset to release those negative thoughts and forgive those people for their false thinking, after all, they are flawed too. Allow yourself grace and mercy when you're going through growth.

I hope that you were able to identify and unmask your fear reading this book. Assessing yourself is one of the biggest tools you can use to help you get to where you need to be. We often forget to sit down and truly reflect on ourselves. We are always evolving. There are also times we don't recognize when we are dealing with certain issues until someone helps us to identify it.

There are many facets of fear. As the book laid out, there are several character traits that are deeply rooted in fear. I added a different perspective so that you can ultimately see that if you can overcome fear, you can overcome any obstacle. We know that fear can cause immobilization. However, what I want you to understand the most is you have to learn to keep moving. The more you move, the further you will go.

So, what's the "F" in F$#%? Face it.

"Just because you feel fear doesn't mean you can't do it. Do it afraid" –Joyce Meyers.

The reality is, when you begin to move toward your

goals, despite fear, your action will allow you to overcome fear. When you continue to take action, you'll gain clarity and creativity. The power of moving is greater than the idea of fear.

Additional Resources

F$#% FEAR WORKSHEET- bit.ly/worksheetffear

Books: https://bit.ly/janelljonesbooks

Courses: https://bit.ly/janelljonescourses

Website: www.janelljonesempowers.com

Podcast: http://bit.ly/girlyougotthispodcast2

About The Author

Janell Jones is on a mission to help others take back their lives through the power of loving themselves and knowing their worth. Janell received an associate's degree in psychology, bachelors and Master's degree in social work, and an honorary doctored degree in healthcare and leadership. Even after she landed what she thought was her "dream job" and made a good home for her children, she discovered a deeper dream buried within her—Janell made the decision to follow her passion.

She started a business and wrote the book that was burning inside her. Today, Janell is a certified life-coach, published author, social work professional, founder of a publishing company, and an international speaker. Janell shares the amazing story of how she took the leap that awakened her to her purpose and destiny.

www.ingramcontent.com/pod-product-compliance
Lightning Source LLC
Chambersburg PA
CBHW071038080526
44587CB00015B/2681